# The Patchsmith
# CHRISTMAS MUG RUGS

## by Amanda Weatherill

PATCHSMITH CHRISTMAS MUG RUGS
Text and Pattern copyright © 2013 Amanda Weatherill
Paperback Edition Published: 2014
All rights reserved.

No part of this publication may be reproduced, stored in retrieval system, copied in any form or by any means, electronic, mechanical, photocopying, recording or otherwise transmitted without prior permission in writing from the author.

The designs and projects in this book are copyright and must not be made for sale without prior permission from the author, Amanda Weatherill.

The information given in this book is presented in good faith. The author has made every effort to ensure that the instructions in this book are accurate. Please study the instructions and diagrams for the pattern you wish to make. However, no warranty is given, nor results guaranteed as responsibility cannot be taken for the choice of fabric, tools, human error or personal skill.

# CONTENTS

**GENERAL INSTRUCTIONS**
Fabric, techniques and binding ............. 1

GIFTS MUG RUG ............................... 7

REINDEER MUG RUG ........................ 13

COUNTRY TREE MUG RUG .............. 17

TREE DECORATIONS MUG RUG ....... 21

THREE TREES MUG RUG ................... 24

SNOWMAN MUG RUG ......................... 27

ROBIN'S GIFT MUG RUG ..................... 31

MISTLETOE MUG RUG ....................... 35

SANTA'S WHEEL MUG RUG ............... 38

THREE KINGS MUG RUG ................... 41

About the Author .................................. 45

GENERAL INSTRUCTIONS

## Before you start
Read through all instructions for the pattern of your choice before beginning.
Fabric requirements and cutting directions are given at the beginning of each pattern.
All seam allowances are ¼" and are included in cutting sizes.
Press seam allowance towards the darker fabric unless stated otherwise.

## Using the patterns
Each pattern has been created as a stand-alone unit to allow you to work quickly and easily. The appliqué diagrams are located with the individual patterns and are at the correct size. Some of the appliqué images have been reversed – you should trace them exactly as shown on the appliqué sheet – they will be the right way round on your finished mug rug.

## Fabric Choices
Due to their size, mug rugs are an excellent use for some of those fabric scraps left over from a bigger project. The largest piece of fabric you will require for any of the projects in this book is 12" x 9" and that is for the backing. The appliqué detailing uses much smaller pieces – perfect for scraps, charm squares or recycled fabrics.

I have just two requirements from my fabric: firstly it has to be 100% cotton and secondly it must be colour-fast. If you stick to these two rules you will be fine.
If you are new to mug rugs or small quilts then a good way to build up a fabric stash is to use pre-cuts. These can be found in any fabric shop. It is also handy to have a few fat-quarters (quarter of a yard) ready for background and backing. A good background fabric will have a small print and not be too bold in design or colour.

Do not neglect the backing fabric either. There is a tendency to use fabric that we are not so keen on or do not like, in the belief that it will not be seen. However, if you are gifting a mug rug then use a nice piece of fabric or, if you have the time, patch the back. I like to use fabric for the backing that reflects the front design. Therefore, for many of the designs in this book I have used a Christmas print for the backing.

Mug rugs are meant to be fun – they give you the opportunity to play with pattern and colour – so remember this and try out some unusual combinations. You never know when you'll discover a new favourite group of colours or pattern.

## Appliqué

All patterns in this book use the quick and easy fusible method of appliqué. You will need lightweight fusible webbing (i.e. Bondaweb, Vleisofix, Wonderweb or similar).

Each pattern includes appliqué instructions but here they are in a little more detail.

1.   Trace around the appliqué shapes onto the paper side of the fusible webbing. Fusible webbing has two sides – one smooth (paper side) and one rough (webbing side). Trace the design onto the smooth paper side.

**Note:** Some of the shapes have been reversed – trace them exactly as shown – they will be the right way round on the finished mug rug.

2.   Cut out the shapes roughly (do not cut out accurately at this stage). You should leave approximately ¼" free around each shape when cutting out.

3.   Follow the manufacturer's instructions to iron the fusible webbing cut outs onto the WRONG side of your chosen fabrics. The rough (webbing) side should be facing the WRONG side of your fabric. DO NOT IRON THE WEBBING SIDE – YOU WILL RUIN YOUR IRON.

4.   Allow the fabric to cool completely before cutting out the shapes accurately along the traced lines.

5.   Peel the paper away from the fusible webbing/fabric. This will leave a layer of glue on the fabric cut outs. Position the fabric cut outs, with the glue side facing down,

onto the RIGHT side of the mug rug. Use the appliqué diagram and photo as a guide to their placement and make a note of any pieces which overlap. When happy with the arrangement, fuse the pieces in place according to manufacturer's instructions.

TIP: *Always leave enough room between the appliqué and the edge of the mug rug to allow for binding.*

6.      Finally stitch the appliqué shapes in position by hand or machine. You can use a running stitch, blanket stitch or any decorative stitch your prefer. It is important to stitch the pieces in place so that they do not come off when the mug rug is laundered.

## Quilting

Mug rugs can be quilted with any thick material you have to hand – it doesn't have to be batting or wadding. You can use old towelling or layers of flannel. Whatever you use should be washable and thick enough to protect the table from hot cups/liquid. I have used both natural and synthetic materials ranging in thickness from 2 oz to 4 oz.
*Tip: If your batting is too thick and fluffy, place a piece of fabric over it and press it firmly with a hot iron to flatten it.*

The designs in this book **have not** been created to be used as hot pads.

When it comes to quilting the finished mug rug, you can make it as simple or as complex as you like, whether by machine or by hand. You can even leave the mug rug un-quilted if you wish.

To prepare your mug rug for quilting, lay the backing material with WRONG side facing up, lay the batting on top and finally lay the mug rug with RIGHT side facing up on top of both. (In effect you have a sandwich of batting between the backing material and the mug rug top.) Baste or pin all three layers together, ensuring that the backing and top remain flat and smooth. Quilt as preferred (hand or machine) and quilt around each appliqué shape. Once all quilting has been completed, trim backing and batting level with the mug rug top.

## Binding Methods

There are many different ways to finish your mug rugs. For all the patterns within this book I have used 1¼" wide cotton strips as binding but you could use bias binding if you prefer. I do not cut my binding on the bias unless I want a particular look i.e. a diagonal stripe. All binding is cut from ordinary quilters' fabric.

You can use any binding method you are familiar with or prefer. I have given instructions here for my two preferred methods.

### Single Fold Binding

1. Cut four binding strips each measuring 2" longer than the sides of your mug rug i.e. if your mug rug is 6" x 9" cut two 1¼" x 8" and two 1¼" x 11" strips.

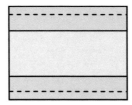

2. With RIGHT sides together stitch a binding strip to the top and bottom of your mug rug. Trim the excess binding to match the width of the mug rug. Press the binding away from the mug rug.

3. Repeat with the two remaining binding strips to the sides of the mug rug. Trim the excess binding to match the length of mug rug. Press the binding away from the mug rug.

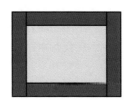

4. Fold the binding round to the back of the rug. Turn under ¼" on the outside edge of the binding slip stitch the binding in place being careful not to stitch through to the front of the rug.

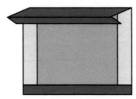

## Mitred Binding

This method of binding creates a mitred corner finish to your mug rug.
*Note: You will need one continuous length of 1¼" wide binding – this can be constructed from strips sewn together. For all mug rugs in this book one yard (36") should be sufficient.*

1. Fold the short end of your binding strip into a triangle and align to your mug rug, RIGHT sides together, as shown (this will create a neat start/finish to your binding). Stitch the binding to the side of your mug rug but stop when you are ½" away from the first corner. Cut the thread and take the rug out of the machine.

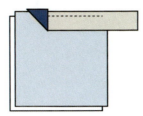

2. Now fold the binding up and away from the mug rug as shown. This will create a triangular fold in the binding at the corner.

3. Hold the triangular fold (or pin it) before folding the binding down over it, aligning the edge of the binding with the side of the mug rug. Pin to secure in place. Stitch the binding along the side from top to bottom, stopping once again when you are ½" away from the next corner.

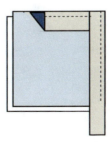

4. Repeat this process for all four corners. Continue stitching the binding until you are 1" past the beginning.

5. Fold the binding to the back of the mug rug, turning under ¼" on the raw edge. Slip-stitch the binding in place, over the line of machine stitching, on the back of the mug rug. Make sure you do not stitch through to the front.

## Buttons, Ribbon and Trim

Mug rugs are functional little quilts. Cups and mugs are placed on them along with cookies, cakes and biscuits. Spills and drips are unavoidable and as such, it is important that mug rugs can be laundered. Ribbons, labels and trims can add an extra dimension to little quilts but make sure they are suitable for laundering and ironing prior to adding them to your quilt.

It is also important that cups are steady when placed on a mug rug. Buttons seldom cause a cup to topple unless they are particularly large or have a shank therefore, for all patterns in this book you should select buttons that lie flat and are relatively small (½" in diameter or smaller). If you do not have a suitable button you can use a circle of felt/fabric in its place.

## Hanging Corner Triangles

Some mug rugs are so pretty that you may wish to hang one on your workroom wall rather than have it on your desk. Or perhaps you already have one on your desk but want to make another.

Hanging corner triangles are a great way to achieve this. They enable you to hang a mug rug or small quilt using only one tack in the wall.
All that is needed is two 3" squares of fabric. Fold the squares in half diagonally, with WRONG sides together and press. After quilting and trimming your mug rug and prior to attaching the binding, pin the triangles to the top corners on the back of your quilt as shown.

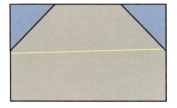 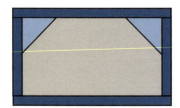

Complete the binding as detailed in the pattern and, as you stitch the binding in place you will also be stitching the triangles in place.

To hang your mug rug all you need to do is insert a pencil or chopstick (trimmed if necessary) into the two corners and hang it on a small tack/nail.

# GIFTS MUG RUG
(Finished Size: 9" x 5½")

Do you like to wrap your gifts neatly with bows and ribbons or are you happy to pop them into a little gift bag? With this mug rug you have the option for both – a holly-decorated gift bag or ribbon-decorated parcels.

### Fabric Requirements:

*For the Gift Bag/Parcels background*:
One 4" x 5½" rectangle

*For the Patched Block*:
- **Fabric A:** Two 1½" squares
  Two 1½" x 3½" rectangles
- **Fabric B:** One 1½" square for centre
  Two 1½" x 3½" rectangles
  Two 1½" x 5½" rectangles

*You will also need*:
- Various scraps for Gift Bag/Parcels
- 2" square of green felt for holly (gift bag option)
- One small button
- Small label (optional)
- One rectangle 11" x 7" cotton fabric for backing
- One rectangle 11" x 7" of lightweight batting
- 6" square fusible webbing (i.e. Bondaweb/Wonder Under)
- 1 yard of 1¼" binding fabric (i.e. bias binding or cotton strips)
- Stranded Embroidery Cotton

## Mug Rug Construction

1. With RIGHT sides together stitch a 1½" **fabric A** square to either side of the centre 1½" **fabric B** square as shown. Press. Unit should measure 3½" x 1½".

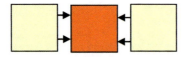

2. Stitch a 3½" x 1½" **fabric A** rectangle to the top and bottom of the patched unit. Press. Unit should measure 3½" square.

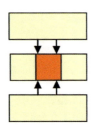

3. Stitch a 3½" x 1½" **fabric B** rectangle to both sides of the patched unit. Press. Unit should measure 5½" x 3½".

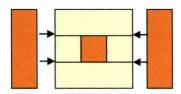

4. Stitch a 5½" x 1½" **fabric B** rectangle to the top and bottom of the patched unit to complete the patched 5½" block. Press.

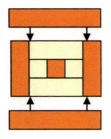

5. With RIGHT sides together stitch the 4" x 5½" background rectangle to the right-hand side of the patched block. If you are using a label then you should position it between the right sides of the two units and stitch in place at the same time as stitching the two units together. Press.

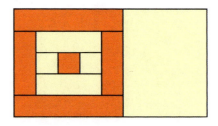

6. From the appliqué diagram, trace the gift bag and holly leaf, or parcel templates onto the paper side of the fusible webbing. Cut out the shapes roughly - **do not** cut out accurately along the lines at this stage. Following the manufacturer's instructions iron the fusible webbing cut-outs onto the WRONG side of your chosen fabrics (the holly leaf should be fused onto green felt).

7. Allow to cool then cut out the shapes accurately along the traced lines. Peel the paper from each shape. Position the pieces onto the mug rug as shown on the appliqué page. Leave **at least** ½" between the appliqué pieces and the edge of the mug rug and remember to allow for the binding when positioning the pieces. When happy with the placement, iron to fuse the pieces in place.

Tip: *If applying ribbon or trim you can tuck the ends of the ribbon behind the appliqué piece before fusing in place. Remember to make sure all ribbon/trim is suitable (see Buttons, Ribbons and Trim in General Instructions).*

8. Stitch the appliqué pieces in place by hand or machine.

9. Lay the 11" x 7" backing rectangle, **wrong** side facing up and place the batting on top. Position the mug rug centrally on top with **right** side facing up. Baste or pin all three layers together, ensuring that the backing and top remain flat and smooth.

10. Quilt around the gift bag/parcels and add a handle to the top of the bag as shown on the appliqué page. (If making the parcel version you may wish to quilt a bow on the top of the parcel stack.) Quilt in the ditch on all seams and add any additional quilting as desired.

11. Once all quilting has been completed, trim backing and batting to the same size as the mug rug top. Bind the mug rug using the binding method of your choice. *I used a single-fold 1¼" binding.* (See Binding Methods in General Instructions.)

12. Finally add a small button to the top of the holly or to the gift tag. Add a bow to the top of the parcel stack if desired.

Design Suggestion:
*This design is great for other occasions too, such as a birthday or anniversary. Add store-brought flowers and trim for a totally different look.*

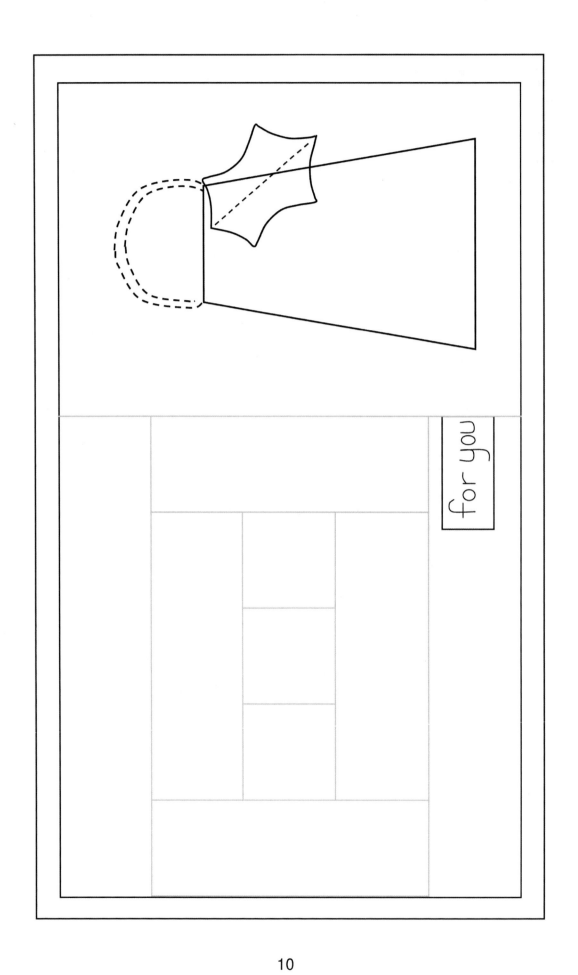

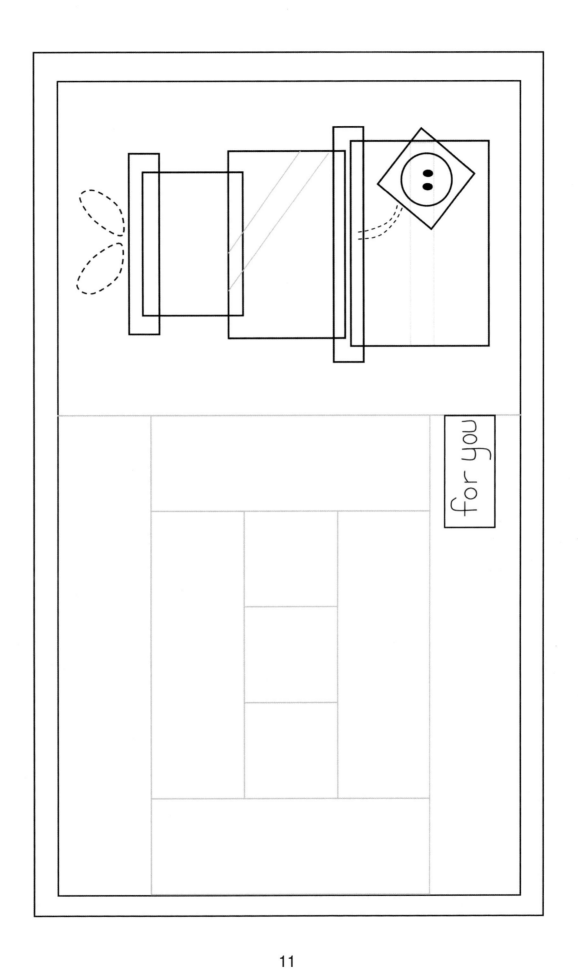

# REINDEER MUG RUG

(Finished Size: 9" x 5½")

These reindeer are taking a rest after another busy evening whizzing around the world pulling a sleigh and a little guy in a red suit. Christmas is a busy time for everybody so to make sure you are not whizzing around reversing diagrams I have included appliqué diagrams with the reindeer facing in both directions. All you need to do is pick your fabrics and decide whether one of your reindeer might have a red nose!

### Fabric Requirements:

*For the background:*
One 9" x 5½" rectangle

*For the Reindeer:*
Two 4" squares for the bodies
Two 2" x 3" rectangles for heads and legs

*You will also need:*
Scraps of fabric for blankets, legs, noses and antlers
One rectangle 11" x 8" cotton fabric for backing
One rectangle 11" x 8" of lightweight batting
8" square fusible webbing (i.e. Bondaweb/Wonderweb)
1 yard of 1¼" binding fabric (i.e. bias binding or cotton strips)
Stranded Embroidery Cotton

NOTE: *You have the option of the reindeer facing left or right on your finished mug rug. Select the appliqué diagram with the reindeer in the opposite direction to your chosen direction i.e. if you want the reindeer facing right on the finished mug rug you should use the appliqué diagram with the reindeer facing left.*

## Mug Rug Construction

1. Trace around all shapes from the appliqué diagram onto the paper side of the fusible webbing. Cut out the shapes roughly - **do not** cut out accurately along the traced lines at this stage. Following the manufacturer's instructions iron the fusible webbing cut-outs onto the WRONG side of your chosen fabrics.

2. Allow to cool then cut out the shapes accurately along the traced lines. Peel the paper from each shape. *Tip: If you intend to embroider the blankets you may wish to do this before fusing them in place.*

Position the fabric shapes onto your mug rug background using the appliqué diagram and photo as a guide. Ensure that all shapes are **at least** ¼" from the edge of the mug rug to allow for binding. When happy with the arrangement, iron to fuse in place. Stitch the appliqué pieces in place by hand or machine.

3. Using two strands of black embroidery thread and a simple overstitch (or French knot) create the reindeers' eyes. Alternatively you could use a permanent fabric marker pen (test it on a scrap of fabric before marking the eyes on the actual mug rug top.) Add any additional stitching as desired. *I added a running stitch motif to each blanket as indicated on the appliqué diagram.*

4. Lay the 11" x 8" backing rectangle, **wrong** side facing up and place the batting on top. Position the mug rug centrally on top with **right** side facing up. Baste or pin all three layers together, ensuring that the backing and top remain flat and smooth. Quilt around each reindeer by hand or machine. Add any additional quilting as preferred.

5. Once all quilting has been completed, trim backing and wadding to the same size as the mug rug top.

6. Bind the mug rug using the binding method of your choice. I used 1¼" single fold binding. (See Binding Methods in General Instructions.)

Tip: *Pick fun fabric for the blankets and leave out the embroidery.*

# COUNTRY TREE MUG RUG

(Finished Size: 9" x 5½")

This is the first of three tree designs in this book because a Christmas just isn't Christmas without trees. This pattern introduces you to my strip-applique method which will have you creating these country patched trees quickly and easily. And if you fancy making one to keep and one to give just double the length of the strips of fabric and batch make the trees.

## Fabric Requirements:

*For the background*:
Two 4¾" x 5½" rectangles

*For the tree*:
Three 4" x 3" rectangles
**OR** eleven 4" x 1" strips from various fabrics if patching the tree

*For the hearts*:
Three 3" squares

*You will also need*:
Two 2" squares of brown fabric for trunks
One rectangle 11" x 7" cotton fabric for backing
One rectangle 11" x 7" of lightweight batting
8" square fusible webbing (i.e. Bondaweb/Wonder Under)
1 yard of 1¼" binding fabric (i.e. bias binding or cotton strips)
Stranded Embroidery Cotton

## Mug Rug Construction

1. With RIGHT sides together stitch the two background rectangles together, along the 5½" length, to create a mug rug top measuring 9" x 5½". Press.

2. PATCHED TREES: With RIGHT sides together stitch the 1" strips of fabric together along the 4" length to make patched units.

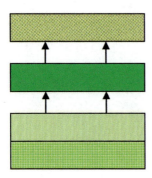

You will need to stitch four strips together for the bottom and middle tree sections and three strips for the top tree section. Press each unit.

3. Trace all shapes from the appliqué diagram onto the paper side of the fusible webbing. Cut out the shapes roughly - **do not** cut out accurately along the lines at this stage. Following the manufacturer's instructions, iron the fusible cut-outs onto the WRONG side of your chosen fabrics.
*Note: If you are patching the trees then fuse the tree cut-outs onto the WRONG side of the patched units.*

4. Allow to cool before cutting out the shapes accurately along the traced lines. Carefully peel the paper from each shape taking care not to pull the patched tree seams apart.

5. Position the pieces onto the background using the appliqué placement diagram as your guide. With the exception of the trunk, make sure each piece is at least ½" from the edge. The top section of the tree lies on top of the middle section and the middle section lies on top of the bottom section.

6. When happy with the placement, fuse the pieces into position. Stitch the shapes in place by hand or machine.

7. Add any ribbon or trim to the tree as desired.

8. Lay the 11" x 7" backing rectangle, **wrong** side facing up and place the batting on top. Position the mug rug centrally on top with **right** side facing up. Baste or pin all three layers together, ensuring that the backing and top remain flat and smooth. Quilt around each appliqué piece and quilt in the ditch on the middle seam.

9. Using two strands of embroidery thread, stitch a hanging cord from each heart to the top of the mug rug. Add any additional stitching as desired.

10. Once all quilting has been completed, trim backing and batting to the same size as the mug rug top. Bind the mug rug using the binding method of your choice. *I used a single-fold 1¼" binding.* (See Binding Methods in General Instructions.)

Design Suggestion:
*Create a reverse image of background and tree colours:*

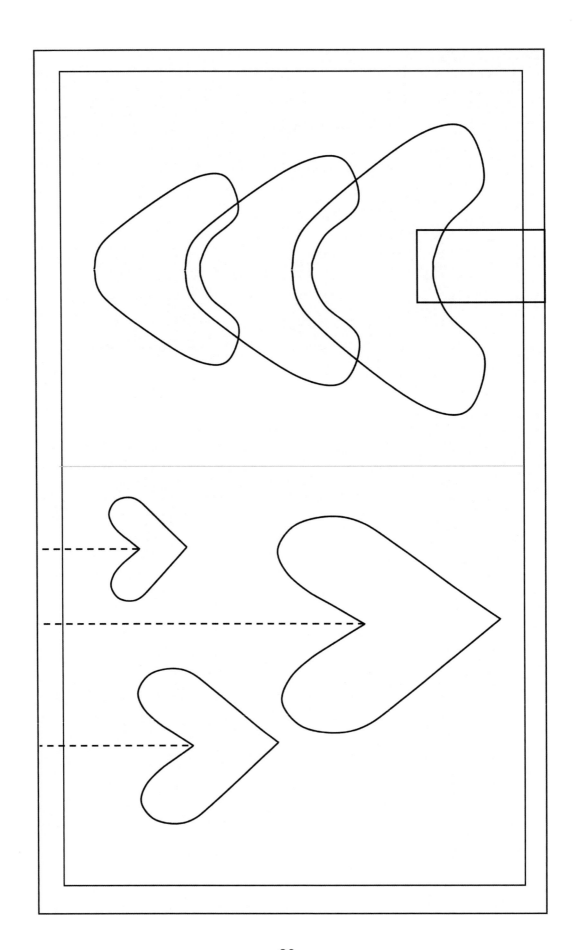

# TREE DECORATIONS MUG RUG
(Finished Size: 9" x 5½")

What decorations do you like hanging from your Christmas tree?
With this pattern you can choose the baubles shown here for a crisp, modern look or replace them with hearts from the Country Tree pattern, for a cosy, homely feel. Either way this pattern will ensure your fabric scraps aren't hanging around for long.

## Fabric Requirements:

*For the background*:
Two 4¾" x 5½" rectangles

*For the tree*:
One 5" square
One 2" square of brown 'trunk' fabric

*For the baubles*:
Six 2½" x 1½" rectangles (two for each bauble)
Two 2½" x ¾" strips of contrast fabric
One 2½" x 1" strip of contrast fabric
Note: If you prefer not to patch the larger baubles then you will need three 2½" squares of fabric.

*You will also need*:
Scraps of fabric for small tree baubles
One rectangle 11" x 7" cotton fabric for backing
One rectangle 11" x 7" of lightweight batting
8" square fusible webbing (i.e. Bondaweb/Wonder Under)
1 yard of 1¼" binding fabric (i.e. bias binding or cotton strips)

## Mug Rug Construction

1. With RIGHT sides together stitch the two background rectangles together to create a mug rug top measuring 9" x 5½". Press.

2. To make the small and medium sized baubles stitch the two 2½" x ¾" contrast strips between two pairs of 2½" x 1½" bauble rectangles. Press seams open.

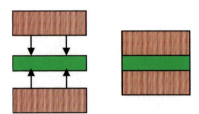

3. Repeat with the 2½" x 1" contrast strip and the remaining two 2½" x 1½" rectangles for the larger bauble. Press seams open.

4. From the appliqué diagram, trace the baubles onto the paper side of the fusible webbing.
*Tip: You may find it helpful to mark the center lines onto each tracing.*

Cut out the shapes roughly - **do not** cut out accurately along the lines at this stage. Following the manufacturer's instructions iron the fusible webbing cut-outs onto the WRONG side of the patched units ensuring the contrast strips are centred as shown.

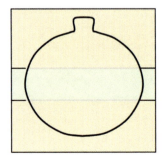

5. From the appliqué diagram, trace the tree, trunk and tree baubles onto the paper side of the fusible webbing. Cut out the shapes roughly and following the manufacturer's instructions iron the fusible webbing cut-outs onto the WRONG side of your chosen fabrics as before.

6. Allow to cool then cut out the shapes accurately along the traced lines. Carefully peel the paper from each shape taking care not to pull the bauble seams apart. Position the shapes onto the mug rug as shown on the appliqué page. Remember to allow for the binding when positioning the pieces and leave **at least** ½" between the tree and the bauble shapes. When happy with the placement, fuse the shapes in place.

7. Stitch all pieces in place by hand or machine. Add any additional stitching as desired. You can stitch the bauble hanging threads in place now or add them when you quilt.

8. Lay the 11" x 7" backing rectangle, **wrong** side facing up and place the batting on top. Position the mug rug centrally on top with **right** side facing up. Baste or pin all three layers together, ensuring that the backing and top remain flat and smooth. Quilt around all shapes and quilt in the ditch on the central seam.

9. Using two strands of embroidery thread, stitch a hanging cord from each bauble to the top of the mug rug/tree. Add any additional quilting as desired.

10. Once all quilting has been completed, trim backing and batting to the same size as the mug rug top. Bind the mug rug using the binding method of your choice. (See Binding Methods.)

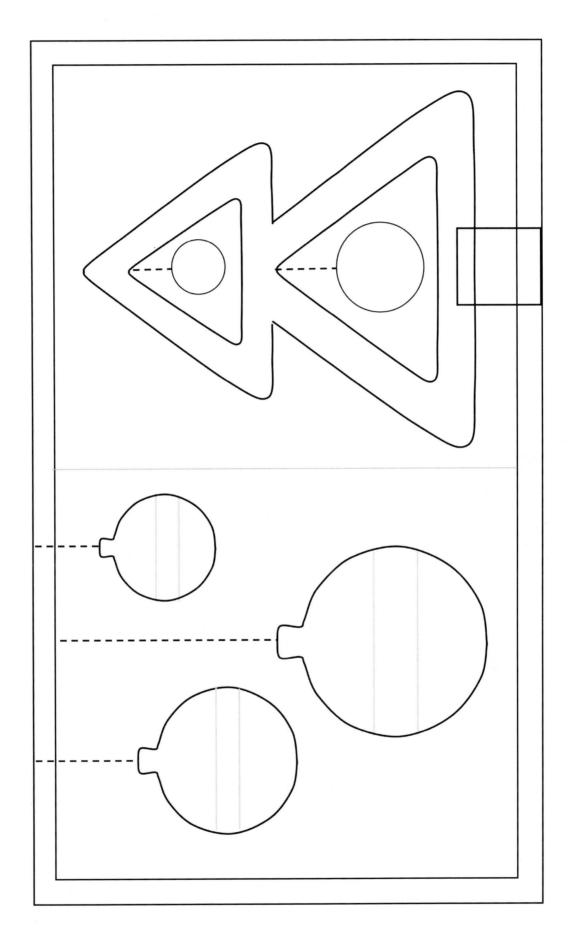

# THREE TREES MUG RUG
(Finished Size: 9" x 5½")

Interlocking trees create a simple yet effective woodland mug rug. Shown here in Christmas checks with country hearts this mug rug would also make the perfect desk addition for Valentines Day.

## Fabric Requirements:

*For the background*:
One 9" x 5½" rectangle

*For the trees:*
Three 5" squares
One 4" square of brown 'trunk' fabric

*For the hearts:*
One 5" square

*You will also need*:
One rectangle 11" x 7" cotton fabric for backing
One rectangle 11" x 7" of lightweight batting
8" square fusible webbing  (i.e. Bondaweb/Wonder Under)
1 yard of 1¼" binding fabric (i.e. bias binding or cotton strips)
Stranded Embroidery Cotton

## Mug Rug Construction

1. From the appliqué diagram, trace the tree, trunk and hearts three times, onto the paper side of the fusible webbing. Make sure to mark a line on two of the tree tracings as indicated by the red dotted line on the appliqué diagram. Cut out the shapes roughly - **do not** cut out accurately along the lines at this stage. Following the manufacturer's instructions iron the fusible webbing cut-outs onto the WRONG side of your chosen fabrics.

2. Allow to cool then cut out the shapes accurately along the traced lines. Decide upon the placement of the trees and cut along the marked dotted line on the left and middle trees ONLY. **The right-hand tree is left uncut.** Carefully peel the paper from each tree taking care not to pull the trees out of shape.

3. Position the trunks and trees onto the background rectangle overlapping the bottom of each tree so that the cut section lies underneath the adjoining tree as shown. Remember to allow for the binding when positioning the pieces and leave **at least** ½" between the trees and the edge of the mug rug. When happy with the placement, fuse the shapes in place.

4. Stitch all pieces in place by hand or machine. Add any additional stitching as desired. You can stitch the heart hanging threads in place now or add them when you quilt.

5. Lay the 11" x 7" backing rectangle, **wrong** side facing up and place the batting on top. Position the mug rug centrally on top with **right** side facing up. Baste or pin all three layers together, ensuring that the backing and top remain flat and smooth. Quilt around all shapes.

6. If you have not already added hanging cords add them using two strands of embroidery thread. Add any additional quilting as desired.

7. Once all quilting has been completed, trim backing and batting to the same size as the mug rug top. Bind the mug rug using the binding method of your choice. *I used a single-fold 1¼" binding.* (See Binding Methods in General Instructions.)

# SNOWMAN MUG RUG
(Finished Size: 9" x 6½")

We've all heard the saying, cold hands – warm heart. This cheery snowman is so warm-hearted even the birds flock to him. And you will too with his Victorian flat cap and colourful Christmas scarf. The snowflake side bars are created using quick pieced patchwork making this the perfect Christmas resting place for a cup of good cheer.

## Fabric Requirements:

*For the background:*
One 6" x 6½" rectangle
Six 1½" x 4" strips from different fabrics

*For the Snowman:*
One 5" square of white felt/thick cotton

*You will also need:*
Scraps of fabric for bird, scarf, hat, buttons, arms and nose
One rectangle 11" x 8" cotton fabric for backing
One rectangle 11" x 8" of lightweight batting
8" square fusible webbing (i.e. Bondaweb/Wonder Under)
1 yard of 1¼" binding fabric (i.e. bias binding or cotton strips)
Stranded Embroidery Cotton

## Mug Rug Construction

1. With right sides together stitch the six 1½" x 4" strips together along the 4" length as shown below. Unit should measure 6½ x 4". Press.

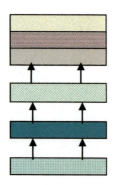

2. Cut this unit in half to create two 6½ x 2" strips. Press.

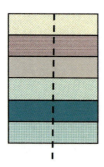

3. Stitch a 2" side strip to each 6½" side of the central rectangle. Press. The mug rug top should measure 9" x 6½".

4. From the appliqué page, trace around each appliqué shape onto the paper side of the fusible webbing (Bondaweb/Wonderweb). Note: The bird, hat and scarf have been reversed – trace them exactly as shown.

5. Cut out the shapes roughly - **do not** cut out accurately along the lines at this stage. Following the manufacturer's instructions iron the fusible webbing cut-outs onto the WRONG side of your chosen fabrics. The snowman body should be fused onto white felt or thick white cotton.
*Tip: If you are using white cotton fabric instead of felt for the snowman you can fuse two pieces of fabric together to create a thicker fabric. This will stop the background showing through.*

6. Allow to cool then cut out the shapes accurately along the traced lines. Peel the paper from each shape. Position all pieces onto the mug rug as shown in the photo and on the appliqué page. Leave **at least** ¼" between the appliqué pieces and the edge of the mug rug. The arms lie under the main body. All other pieces lie on top. When happy with the placement, iron to fuse the pieces in place.
*Tip: I fused and stitched the snowman and arms in place before adding the additional pieces.*

7. Stitch the shapes in place by hand or machine.
*I used one strand of cotton when stitching the nose in place to minimize the impact of the stitching.*

8. Using two strands of black embroidery thread and a simple overstitch create the bird's eye, beak and the snowman's eyes. The snowman's smile is created using black thread and a simple running stitch. Add any additional stitching as desired.

9. Lay the 11" x 8" backing rectangle, **wrong** side facing up and place the batting on top. Position the appliquéd panel centrally on top with **right** side facing up. Baste or pin all three layers together, ensuring that the backing and top remain flat and smooth. Quilt around the snowman and add any additional quilting as desired.
*I quilted in the ditch on all seams before quilting snowflakes on the side strips.*

10. Once all quilting has been completed, trim backing and wadding to the same size as the mug rug top.

11. Bind the mug rug using the binding method of your choice. *I used a 1¼" wide single-fold binding.* (See Binding Methods in General Instructions.)

## SNOWMAN APPLIQUÉ

30

# ROBIN'S GIFT MUG RUG
(Finished Size: 9½" x 5")

Robins are such friendly birds – happy to search for scraps all winter long. Join the robin and gather up some fabric scraps to create this lovely little mug rug with its mock envelope – perfect for holding a seasonal gift card or small treat.
And should you wish to make this little quilt for another occasion then just change the robin to a bluebird or a blackbird.

### Fabric Requirements:

*For the background*:
One 9½" x 5" rectangle

*For the Robin:*
One 4" square of brown fabric
4" x 2" strip of red fabric
2" square for wing
Scrap of fabric for beak

*For the Envelope:*
Two 4½" x 6" rectangles from two different fabrics
Small button (optional)

*You will also need*:
One rectangle 11" x 7" cotton fabric for backing
One rectangle 11" x 7" of lightweight batting
5" square fusible webbing   (i.e. Bondaweb/Wonder Under)
1 yard of 1¼" binding fabric (i.e. bias binding or cotton strips)

## Mug Rug Construction
MAKING THE ROBIN

1. With RIGHT sides together stitch the 4" x 2" strip of red fabric to the bottom of the brown 4" square. Press the seam open.

2. Trace the robin appliqué shapes from the pattern diagram onto the paper side of the fusible webbing. Make sure you mark the dotted line onto the tracing.
*Note: The robin shape has been reversed – trace it exactly as shown. The robin will be the right way round once you have fused it in place.*

3. Cut out the shapes roughly – do not cut out along the traced line at this stage. . Following the manufacturer's instructions iron the fusible robin cut-out onto the WRONG side of the brown/red rectangle aligning the traced line with the seam of the rectangle as shown.

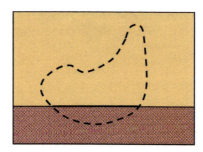

Allow to cool then cut out accurately along the traced line to create one robin redbreast.

MAKING THE ENVELOPE

4. Lay the two 4½" x 6" rectangles together with RIGHT sides facing.

5. Mark the centre point along the top 4½" edge. Mark 2½" down from the top edge on each side. Draw a line from each side mark to the centre mark. Cut along the lines to create a triangle point as shown.

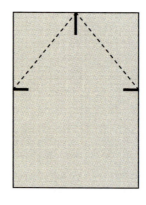 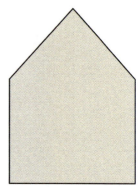

6. Using a ¼" seam stitch the two rectangles together leaving a 2" opening along the bottom edge. Trim the corners before turning the pocket right side out. Turn in ¼" along the opening and press.
*Tip: I used a chopstick to carefully push out the corners.*

7. Fold the pocket to create a mock envelope measuring 4" x 2¾". Press. Topstitch the triangle point in place by stitching 1/8" from the edge as shown in the photo.
*You can add a button to the point of the envelope if you wish but make sure you do not stitch through to the mug rug. The envelope should form a pocket to allow a gift card or note to be inserted into it.*

8. Position the envelope and robin shapes onto the background rectangle as shown on the appliqué page. Leave **at least** ½" between the pieces and the edge of the mug rug to allow for the binding. When happy with the placement, fuse the robin in place and pin the envelope.

9. Stitch the robin in place by hand or machine.

10. Create an eye for the robin by stitching four or five stitches next to each other using two strands of black embroidery cotton.

11. Stitch the envelope in place by top stitching down both sides and along the bottom as shown by the dashed lines on the appliqué page.

12. Lay the 11" x 7" backing rectangle, **wrong** side facing up and place the batting on top. Position the mug rug centrally on top with **right** side facing up. Baste or pin all three layers together, ensuring that the backing and top remain flat and smooth. Quilt around the robin and around the envelope. Add any additional quilting as desired.

13. Once all quilting has been completed, trim backing and batting to the same size as the mug rug top. Bind the mug rug using the binding method of your choice. *I used a single-fold 1¼" binding.* (See Binding Methods in General Instructions.)

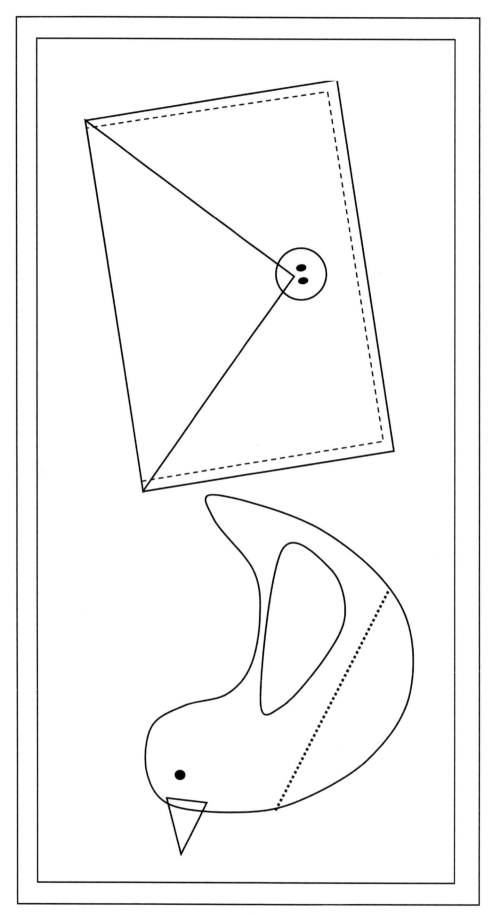

# MISTLETOE MUG RUG
(Finished Size: 9½" x 6½")

Mistletoe is one of the oldest traditions of the Christmas season. Yet there is nothing old about this pattern – unless you choose to use old fabrics that is. Mug rugs are an economical Christmas choice as they use small scraps of fabric and are well suited to up-cycled or recycled fabrics. Shown here in traditional colours, the mistletoe leaves and berry buttons will detract from any imperfections in your patchwork or fabric.

### Fabric Requirements:

*For the background:*
**Fabric A:** Four 2" corner squares
**Fabric B:** Two 2" x 3½" rectangles
Two 6½" x 2" rectangles
**Center:** Four 3½" x 2" rectangles

*For the Mistletoe:*
One 6" square of green fabric for leaves
Four small cream buttons (alternatively you can use cream felt in place of buttons).

*You will also need:*
One rectangle 11" x 8" cotton fabric for backing
One rectangle 11" x 8" of lightweight batting
8" square fusible webbing (i.e. Bondaweb/Wonder Under)
1 yard of 1¼" binding fabric (i.e. bias binding or cotton strips)

## Mug Rug Construction

1. With RIGHT sides together stitch the four center rectangles together as shown. Press. Unit should measure 6½" x 3½".

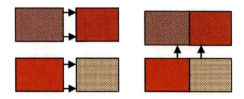

2. Stitch a 6½" x 2" **fabric B** rectangle to the top and bottom of the center unit. Press. Unit should measure 6½" square.

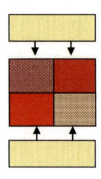

3. Stitch a 2" **fabric A** square to each end of the two remaining 2" x 3½" **fabric B** rectangles. Press. Units should measure 6½" x 2".

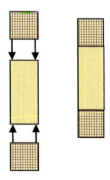

4. Stitch these two units to either side of the patched square to complete the patched mug rug background. The mug rug should measure 9½" x 6½". Press.

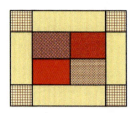

5. From the appliqué diagram, trace twelve mistletoe leaves onto the paper side of the fusible webbing. Cut out the shapes roughly - **do not** cut out accurately along the lines at this stage. Following the manufacturer's instructions iron the fusible webbing cut-outs onto the WRONG side of your chosen fabric.

6. Allow to cool then cut out the leaves accurately along the traced lines. Peel the paper from each shape. Position the leaves onto the mug rug as shown on the appliqué page. Leave **at least** ¼" between the leaves and the edge of the mug rug to allow for the binding. When happy with the placement, iron to fuse the pieces in place.

7. Stitch all pieces in place by hand or machine.

8. Lay the 11" x 8" backing rectangle, **wrong** side facing up and place the batting on top. Position the mug rug centrally on top with **right** side facing up. Baste or pin all three layers together, ensuring that the backing and top remain flat and smooth. Quilt in the ditch on all seams and add any additional quilting as desired.
*I outline quilted around each leaf.*

9. Once all quilting has been completed, trim backing and batting to the same size as the mug rug top. Bind the mug rug using the binding method of your choice. *I used a single-fold 1¼" binding.* (See Binding Methods in General Instructions.)

10. Finally add a button to each corner of the center rectangle.

## MISTLETOE APPLIQUÉ

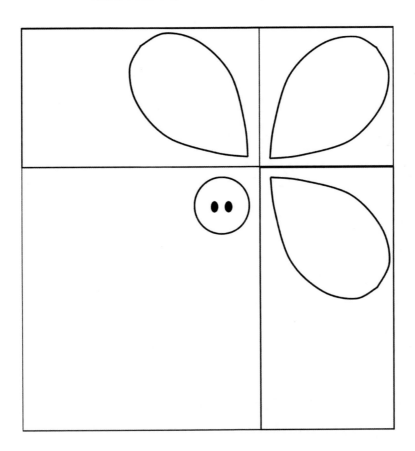

# SANTA'S WHEEL MUG RUG

(Finished Size: 9½" x 5½")

Christmas wouldn't be complete without a visit from Santa. This cheeky chap is one of my oldest designs and has adorned a favourite Christmas wall quilt for many years. Now he is by my side all winter through as he sits on my work table looking after my cuppa and cookie. And while the pinwheel may look complicated it is simply done using quick-fuse appliqué.

## Fabric Requirements:

*For Santa's background*:
One 4½" x 5½" rectangle

*For Santa's Appliqué*:
One 4" square of red fabric for hat and coat
One 3" x 2" black/white check fabric for hat trim
One 1½" square for face
One 3½" square of white felt/thick white cotton for beard and bobble

*For the Pinwheel Background*:
One 5½" square
*For the Pinwheel Appliqué*:
Two 2½" x 6" rectangles red/white stripe fabric

*You will also need*:
One rectangle 11" x 7" cotton fabric for backing
One rectangle 11" x 7" of lightweight batting
8" square fusible webbing (i.e. Bondaweb/Wonder Under)
1 yard of 1¼" binding fabric (i.e. bias binding or cotton strips)
Stranded Embroidery Cotton

## Mug Rug Construction

1. Fold the 5½" pinwheel background square in half diagonally and then half again. Press. Open out the square. The creases will be used to line up the pinwheel appliqué.

2. With **right** sides together, stitch the 5½" pinwheel background square to the left-hand side of the 4½" x 5½" Santa background to create a mug rug top measuring 9½" x 5½". Press.

3. From the appliqué diagram, trace all shapes onto the paper side of the fusible webbing. You will need to trace the pinwheel blades twice. Cut out the shapes roughly - **do not** cut out accurately along the lines at this stage.

4. Following the manufacturer's instructions iron the fusible webbing cut-outs onto the WRONG side of your chosen fabrics. Make sure you position the pinwheel blades at an angle to the stripes of the fabric. The beard and hat bobble should be fused onto white felt or thick cotton to avoid the background showing through.
Tip: *If you do not have felt or thick cotton you can fuse two pieces of white cotton together and treat as one piece to create a thicker fabric.*

5. Allow to cool then cut out the shapes accurately along the traced lines. Peel the paper from each shape.

6. Position the pinwheel blades so that they run along the diagonal creases made at step 1 above. The blades should cross over at the center point. Fuse in place before stitching the blades in position by hand or machine.

7. Position Santa's shoulders, face and beard in place on the right-hand background rectangle. Remember to allow for the binding on the right-hand side and leave **at least** ¼" between the appliqué pieces and the edge of the mug rug with the exception of Santa's shoulders (these should be aligned with the bottom of the mug rug). When happy with the placement, iron to fuse the pieces in place. Stitch the shoulders and beard in place by hand or machine.

8. Repeat this process to appliqué the hat, nose, hat trim and bobble in place as shown on the appliqué page and in the photo.

9. Using two strands of embroidery thread create a smile for Santa using a simple running stitch. The eyes are created using a small overstitch (or French knot).

10. Lay the 11" x 7" backing rectangle, **wrong** side facing up and place the batting on top. Position the mug rug centrally on top with **right** side facing up. Baste or pin all three layers together, ensuring that the backing and top remain flat and smooth. Quilt as desired.

11. Once all quilting has been completed, trim backing and batting to the same size as the mug rug top. Bind the mug rug using the binding method of your choice. *I used a mitred 1¼" binding.* (See Binding Methods)

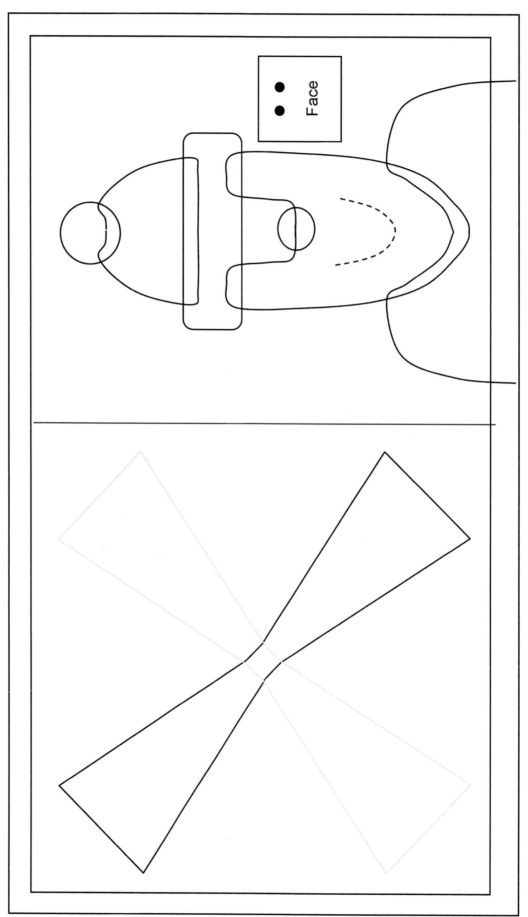

# THREE KINGS MUG RUG
Finished Size 9½" x 6"

The three kings came bearing gifts and so we come to the last of my mug rug gifts for this book. Although this design is not difficult it does require a little bit of patience to get all the pieces into position. The gowns and headgear provide the ideal opportunity to use co-ordinating charm squares from a favourite collection and you can add an extra sparkle to the gift boxes and gowns with gold thread.

Fabric Requirements:

*For the background*:
One 9½" x 6" rectangle

*For the Kings*:
Six 5" squares for gowns and caps
4" square of white felt or thick cotton for beards
4" square of light tan for face and hands
Scraps for crowns and gifts

*You will also need*:
One 11" x 8" rectangle of cotton fabric for backing
One 11" x 8" rectangle of lightweight batting
10" square fusible webbing   (i.e. Bondaweb/Wonderweb)
1 yard of 1¼" binding fabric (i.e. bias binding or cotton strips)
Stranded Embroidery Cotton

## Mug Rug Construction

1. Trace three sets of 'king' shapes from the appliqué diagram onto the paper side of the fusible webbing.
*Note: The pieces have been reversed – trace them exactly as shown.*

2. Cut out the shapes roughly - **do not** cut out accurately along the lines at this stage. Following the manufacturer's instructions, iron the fusible cut-outs onto the WRONG side of your chosen fabrics.
*Tip: If you are not using felt for the beards and you believe the background may show through, you can fuse two pieces of fabric together to create a thicker fabric and treat as one piece.*

3. Allow to cool then cut out the shapes accurately along the traced lines. Peel the paper from each shape.

4. Position the pieces onto the background using the appliqué placement diagram as your guide. Take your time with this step. Make sure each piece is at least ½" from the edge.
*Tip: You may find it easier to position and fuse the middle king first before placing the other two kings either side.* Do not fuse the crown or gift boxes at this stage – these can be applied once all other pieces have been securely stitched in place.

5. When happy with the placement, fuse the pieces into position. Stitch the shapes in place by hand or machine. Repeat this process to position the crowns and gift boxes.

6. Add an eye to each king using two strands of black embroidery thread and a small overstitch or French knot. The moustaches were created using two strands of cream embroidery thread and a simple running stitch.

7. Add detailing on the gift boxes if desired. *I used gold thread to match the fabric.*

8. Lay the backing 11" x 8" rectangle, **wrong** side facing up and place the batting on top. Position the appliquéd mug rug centrally on top with **right** side facing up. Baste or pin all three layers together, ensuring that the backing and top remain flat and smooth. Quilt around each king. Add any additional quilting as desired.

9. Once all quilting has been completed, trim backing and batting to the same size as the mug rug top.

10. Bind the mug rug using the binding method of your choice. I used a 1¼" mitred binding. (See Binding Methods in General Instructions.)

# THREE KINGS APPLIQUÉ

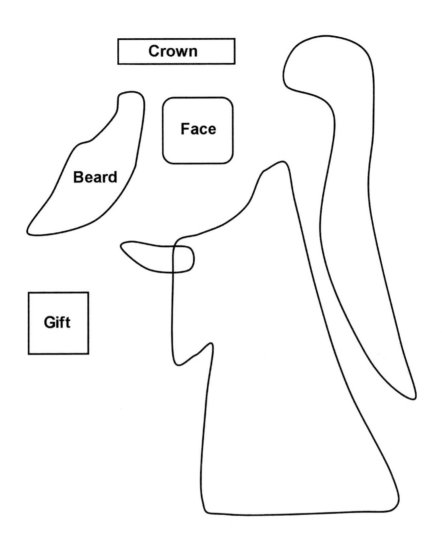

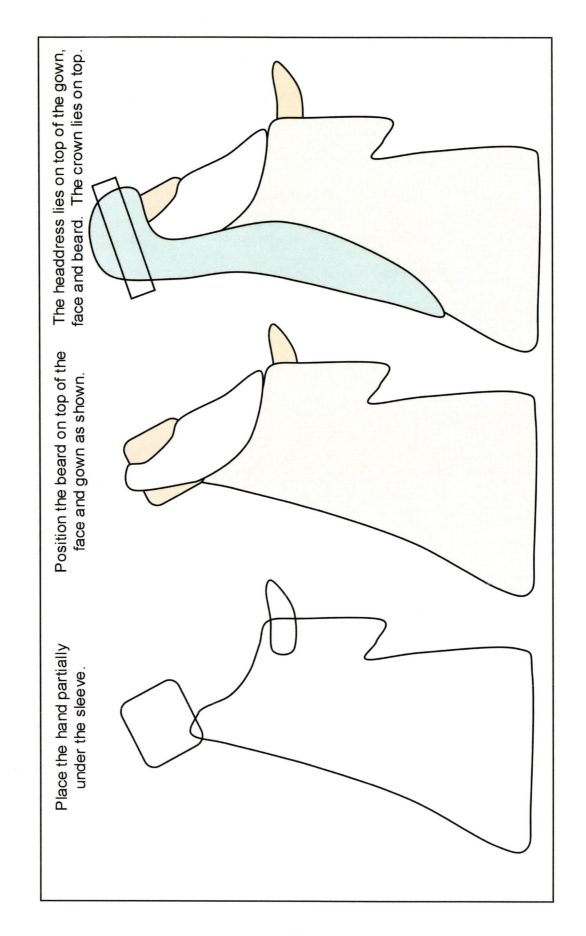

## About the Author

*I am Amanda Weatherill, also known as the Patchsmith. I live in a little village nestled in the Hampshire countryside where I spend my days designing and making mini quilts - they are my passion. My philosophy is simple – share this passion so that everybody has the opportunity to create a little piece of fabric art for their home. Mug rugs are the perfect way to achieve this. Each month I change the mug rug on my desk to reflect the seasons or a special celebratory day. In so doing there is always a reminder close by of my love of sewing and the fun it brings.*

*Join me as I share my quick and easy designs to help you create a life full of fabric, fun and friends.*

*You can find the Patchsmith on Facebook, Flickr, Pinterest and blogger.*

*To find out more about Patchsmith patterns and mug rug making visit* **thepatchsmith.blogspot.co.uk**.

Made in the USA
Lexington, KY
09 January 2016